THE INVESTOR CATCH

Straight talk about investments, fees, risk, and who is poised to profit more—you or your advisor.

Market Advisory Group

With Danny Goolsby, Larry Kloefkorn, Matt Goolsby, and Jonathon McCoy

A MARKET ADVISORY GROUP EDUCATION PUBLICATION

This booklet discusses general concepts for retirement planning and is not intended to provide tax or legal advice. Individuals are urged to consult with their tax and legal professionals regarding these issues.

Market Advisory Group is a registered investment advisory firm of Foundations Investment Advisors, LLC. Advisory services are offered through Foundations Investment Advisors, LLC, an SEC-registered investment advisor.

Printed in the United States of America

First Printing, 2018

Market Advisory Group:
110 E Waterman St Suite 150
Wichita, KS 67202
Phone: 316-252-8707

5000 W 95th St Suite 360
Prairie Village, KS 66207
Phone: 913-730-7749

6300 N Revere Ave Suite 270
Kansas City, MO 64151
Phone: 913-730-7749

TABLE OF CONTENTS

THE INVESTOR CATCH-22

As the story goes, someone once asked Jessie James, "Why do you rob banks?" His reply, "Because that's where the money is." Ask any investor, "Why are you invested in the stock market?" and you'll likely hear the same thing. The market is where all the horsepower is.

While this kind of thinking sounds rational, the market is decidedly irrational. This is what economist John Maynard Keynes was trying to warn investors of when he said, "The market can stay irrational longer than you can stay solvent."

We live during unpredictable times. Pension plans have gone the way of the dinosaur, Social Security benefits are constantly changing, and people continue to live longer thanks to advances in modern medicine. All of this only puts more pressure on the earning potential of your nest egg, yet most investors continue to place all their eggs in market investments, even during retirement, even when losing could very well mean going broke.

But this isn't the full story.

Investors have also been told throughout their working lives to save in vehicles such as 401(k)s and IRAs—but what happens when they get ready to retire? All of this money is going to be taxable, and if you've done a good job saving and happen to be a high-income earner, then a high percentage of your Social Security might also be taxed. From a volatility standpoint, living longer also acts as a kind of risk multiplier: it magnifies the number of times you'll likely go through a market cycle and experience sudden, plunging loss. Longevity also magnifies the likelihood of having a long-term care event.

With all of this stacked up against you, the last thing in the world you need is a brokerage account that is poorly managed, with inappropriate investment classes and high fees. Yet time and time again, that's what we continue to see. People come into our office with their investment account statements, and they are concerned about what they see because it doesn't at all match their needs or expectations. Through no fault of their own, they are paying exorbitant fees for features they often don't need or even know they have, and making choices simply because they don't know that other options and strategies exist. These mistakes are not just expensive; they're harmful to the long-term viability of your nest egg.

And here's the real gotcha: you're going to be on the hook for these fees/taxes/losses/obligations whether you know about them or not. The mistakes are there, even if you choose to keep your head in the sand and your statements sealed in a drawer. So, what can you do about it?

IS THERE AN ESCAPE?

It was the 1961 war novel by Joseph Heller that first coined the phrase "catch-22." The term refers to a kind of paradox whereby escape is impossible. The "damned if you do, damned if you don't" trap that investors face has also to do with the large number of misperceptions and misrepresentations being perpetuated by an industry that relies on their money. You, the investor, are the one who has to do all the saving; if you don't, you'll have nothing to live on during retirement. But the investments you need to generate returns come with sales charges, management fees, and confusing terminology spelled out for you in dry, boring, multipage prospectus reports that would make better doorstops than reading material. (Think about it: if a prospectus has more than

200 pages, who do you think it was written to protect? You, or the investment company?) So what does the rational investor do?

He or she seeks the help of a financial advisor, who in many cases only stands to gain when the investor pays higher fees, and an inherent conflict of interest results. Arthur Levitt, the 25th and longest-serving Chairman of the United States Securities and Exchange Commission (SEC), gave a speech in 2001 on the rights and obligations of America's investors whereby he illustrated the problem of suitability standards. In one example—and there were several—he cited a case reported by the SEC where an investor allegedly paid out more than $168,000 in unnecessary sales charges, even losing some of their principal; meanwhile, over that same period of time, the broker earned himself commissions totaling $210,000.[1]

So many of our clients come from situations where they aren't being serviced and they haven't been taught the pros and cons of the different products they're using. Even the alternative, going it alone and following outdated advice, doggedly holding onto stock portfolios as companies like Enron go down like

[1] https://www.sec.gov/news/speech/spch457.htm

the Titanic, can end up costing you money. The key findings of the 22nd annual Dalbar study also report that in 2015, the average equity mutual fund investor underperformed the S&P 500 by a margin of 3.66 percent.[2] Investors taking a different approach might run for the banks. There, you can purchase bank CDs where you earn so little, you end up doing what we in the industry call "going broke safely."

There is no reason you should have to suffer the indignity of a retirement portfolio that is subpar, earning less than what it could, with balances at a fraction of what you deserve. You do have other options.

PLAN FOR YOUR FUTURE, LIVE YOUR LIFE NOW

As Benjamin Franklin once said, "Beware of little expenses; a small leak will sink a great ship." We're writing this book to help right the ship that is your retirement plan. We're not broker-dealers or financial salesmen or even politicians; we are a group of like-minded fiduciary professionals with over 100 years of combined experience in the financial industry. We believe that putting our clients' best

---

[2] https://www.qidllc.com/wp-content/uploads/2016/02/2016-Dal-bar-QAIB-Report.pdf

interests before our own means operating with the utmost transparency and honesty. To that end, we are presenting you with the facts—the inside story, so to speak—so that you can see for yourself how investment products really work and how *not* to be caught unaware. We'll also tell you stories about real-life individuals such as yourself, people who have made mistakes through no fault of their own—mistakes that we want to help you avoid.

Every advisor out there no doubt has opinions on which investments are best, and which ones have the potential to earn the highest returns. You also no doubt have your own. We're not here to present you with our opinions (although at times we might, in which case we'll let you know). Rather, we consider it our duty as fiduciaries to lay out the facts, not opinions. The more facts you know, the better equipped you'll be to form opinions of your own. This is important, because regardless of how much your broker stands to make in commissions from your investments, nobody cares more about your money than you do.

If you have worked multiple decades to get to where you're at now, if you have arrived and are wondering how to best proceed, we're here to offer you some straight talk about the multiple options that are available to you.

What's the catch?

The only thing that we want you to catch is a retirement, or maybe a fish from the bow of your craft as you sail away into a peaceful sunset.

Here's to a great escape,

~ Market Advisory Group

A little note about how to use this book: Investors come in all shapes and sizes, with different levels of experience. We have tried to make this book welcoming, without it being a dozer for those of you who are savvier savers. **Investment terms** that are in bold are defined in the lower left-hand corner of the page. We've also included an Investor Q&A for quick insights and Gotcha warnings that deliver potentially bad news now so that you can take action before it affects your accounts.

THE INVESTOR CATCH

CHAPTER ONE:
MARKET-BASED INVESTMENTS

KNOW WHAT YOU OWN

"Rule No.1: Never lose money.
Rule No.2: Never forget rule No.1."
~ Warren Buffett

Jerry worked for over 30 years as a high-ranking accountant with Boeing. As someone who was good with shocked numbers, he also handled all his own stock and mutual fund purchasing. He bought into a fund in the technology sector that did well in the 1990s, and so he held onto it, believing in the fund and in the long-term viability of the buy-and-hold strategy.

From 1999 to 2004, the fund lost 73 percent of its value, and Jerry's retirement account plummeted from just over $3 million to just under $810,000. This happened the year before Jerry planned to retire. He was shocked. It was the first devastating loss he'd ever experienced, yet he didn't adjust his strategy or change his approach. Jerry retired and started taking money out of these investment *accounts for his income. His advisor told him to stick with the market, and this reassurance only confirmed Jerry's own belief that the technology sector would continue to advance. But then again in 2008 it fell, and by 2009, his account value was at the bare minimum of what he needed to live on. At that point, he felt he had no other choice but to bail. Jerry cashed out his savings, took his money out of the market, and cobbled together his retirement after losing over $2 million.*

The mistake that Jerry made wasn't investing in the market; it was how he was invested in the market. Not everyone has $2 million to lose, but regardless of the account balances in your retirement portfolio, no one who is near the time of retirement wants to see a 73-percent loss. Investors like Jerry in our story above who experienced loss during what has become known as the Lost Decade are only just now recovering. For those folks who retired during that time, their accounts may never recover.

Jerry retired with a fraction of the benefits he deserved not because he didn't save enough or work hard enough, but because he didn't have the right kind of professional support and

guidance. It was misdirected confidence that kept Jerry improperly invested—that and an investment plan that wasn't in his best interests. This chapter will help identify why.

THE RACECARS OF THE INVESTMENT WORLD

Racecars are designed for aerodynamics. They can hug a curve and go from 0 to 100 miles per hour in 4 seconds flat, while claiming speeds on the racetrack upwards of 200 miles per hour.[3] They are designed specifically to be driven hard and fast for short periods of time, with lots of maintenance in between. Street cars, on the other hand, are designed with completely different goals in mind. Their owners expect comfort and safety, and they rarely if ever exceed 150 miles per hour. These

---

[3] https://www.express.co.uk/sport/f1-autosport/809783/Indy-500-how-fast-top-speed-500-mile-race-200-laps

cars need to run for much longer time periods, and ideally with much less maintenance.

Investments are also designed with different goals in mind. Market-based investments are designed for accumulation. They have the potential for higher rewards, but that also comes with a greater potential for risk. This is one thing that market investments have in common with stock car racing: the potential for cash prizes and spectacular crashes.

To avoid that, investors want to be savvy about the types of investment vehicles they choose and how they are allocated for risk. When making these choices, most people look under the hood of their investments and ask, "How fast can it run?" This is the equivalent of asking, "What is the rate of return?"

There's nothing wrong with assessing the earning potential of your investments, but if that's all you look at, you'll likely not get the vehicle you need. Let's take a tour of the showroom and meet the investments that can provide the horsepower for your portfolio.

Our first stop: stocks.

Irene was an 82-year-old widow in a wheelchair, living off her Social Security income. One day she received a small inheritance from her aunt and wanted to know what she could do with this money to best improve her situation. Her husband had always handled their investments in the past, and so she found an investment advisor willing to make house calls.

The advisor was sitting at her kitchen table when he noticed an entire wall devoted to what looked like several framed stock certificates, displayed rather prominently.

"What's that?" he asked, curious.

"Oh," said Irene, "that's my hubby's pension."

Irene wasn't joking. The stock was for Enron, and it was the only stock they ever owned. All during her working years, Irene was told by her husband, "Look how much our stocks are earning. We're going to receive a stream of income from these dividends, and if we ever need more money, all we have to do is sell." All those years raising three kids and going to work every morning, and he told her they would have it easy someday when they sold off their stock.

Then they retired, Enron went bankrupt, and their stocks became worthless.

STOCKS: Both traditional and dividend-paying stocks can have a place in a well-designed portfolio and may supply the horsepower for growth during the 20 to 30 years that can make up a retirement. When you purchase stock, you are given a piece of ownership in the company—be it a large, small, or medium-size company—and you become a shareholder. In that sense, stocks are a lot like buying a house, in that you hold equity in something tangible (and stocks are sometimes also called equities). As the value of the house/company goes up, the value of your equity/stock goes up. Investors like stocks because they can appreciate, or increase in value. When a company performs well, the price of the company stock rises in value and the investor can make money. When a company depreciates in value due to market volatility, the investor may lose money, which is why stocks are said to have **risk**.

Another reason people like stocks are because of the dividend payments. A company may distribute some of its earnings to its stockholders, but generally speaking, dividend-paying stocks tend to have less of a growth aspect. These are typically large-cap stocks

Risk is the danger or probability of loss.

that grow steadily, albeit at a slower rate. Investors often misunderstand how the yields on dividends work, and they get excited when the price of their stock goes up. Unlike yields, however, *dividends are declared*. **While it's public perception that these dividends typically don't fluctuate and the value of these stocks is a specified monetary amount, there are times when the company may lower or suspend the dividend payout.**

And during bankruptcy, stockholders will stop receiving dividends altogether.[4]

Problems can arise if you have too many of your eggs—or investments—in the basket of one company's stock. We see this often with investors like Irene and her husband in our story above, who participate in their company's profit sharing. Because these investments are done automatically, investors continue buying shares of one company's stock, steadily growing their retirement fund; meanwhile, retirement gets closer and no one asks the question, "How are we positioned for risk?" No matter the stock, you might not want its value to be directly tied to the quality of your future life.

---

[4] https://www.sec.gov/reportspubs/investor-publications/investor-pubsbankrupthtm.html

Investor Q&A: *My stock just split! Should I buy a Ferrari?* Sadly, no. Just because your stock split doesn't mean that it has doubled in value. One benefit may be that more people are able to invest in your stock, but typically its value will not be worth more.

BONDS: Compared to stocks, bonds are traditionally thought of as the safer part of your typical 60/40 stock-and-bond portfolio. When you buy a bond, you are basically loaning money to a company or state municipality in exchange for periodic interest payments, plus the return of the bond's face amount on the date that bond matures. They typically offer a lower rate of return than stocks, but the **principal** on most bonds is thought to be guaranteed.

If interest rates rise, however, you may be forced to sell your bond at a discount. The Federal Reserve has been talking for some time now about the need to normalize interest rates, which for bonds are typically in the neighborhood of 3 to 4 percent. As of the writing of this book, rates continue to remain low, but we may have turned a corner.

Your principal is the base amount of money that you put into an investment.

If interest rates rise as predicted, and you go to sell your lower-rated bonds, you may have to sell at a discount, and it's possible that you won't get all your money back. **In a rising-rate environment, bonds can be as volatile as stocks.** Even though they are perceived as safer and more conservative than stocks, when the interest rates rise, bonds can subject your portfolio to the same type of volatility as stocks.

GOTCHA: Investor alert for callable bonds: corporate bonds are often callable. The best way to explain this is to think about your mortgage. When interest rates go down, the homeowner might like to refinance. With callable bonds, when interest rates change, the corporation is the homeowner, so all the power is in their hands. They can call in the bond, sell it, and refund your money. This gives the company more favorable terms, not you. The investor is left without that income stream, in a position where they have to go back into the market for a new investment while trying not to jeopardize their principal.

INVESTMENT FUNDS: Pooled investments allow investors with similar goals to combine their savings in hopes of benefiting from more diverse purchases and lower individual risk. One of the most common types of investment funds are mutual funds. A mutual fund is an investment company that pools money from many investors and invests it, usually offering built-in diversification and professional management based on specific investment goals. What do mutual funds invest in? Mutual funds are an equity investment just like individual stocks, and you'll recognize the four main fund categories:

- Stock funds
- Bond funds
- Balanced funds (a combination of stocks and bonds)
- Money market funds: short-term investments that are sometimes described as cash equivalents

If you own an IRA with a brokerage company and/or invest in your company's 401(k), then chances are pretty good that you're invested in mutual funds. *Most people invest under the misguided belief that their advisor charges them a small fee of around 1 percent for the privilege of investing in mutual funds.*

Here's the catch, folks: there are many other fees! How many fees? We need a full chapter to understand all the different ways you can be charged fees inside of mutual funds, so stay tuned for what's ahead in Chapter Two.

Investor Q&A: Is there a low-cost option for pooled investments other than mutual funds? Yes!

Exchange-traded funds (ETFs) are pooled investments like mutual funds, but they typically have lower operating expenses, no loads (or sales charges), and no 12b-1 fees.

When Joe was 58, he went to his advisor and told him, "I'm going to be retiring in the next few years. What can you get me in the way of guarantees? I don't want to lose any of my income to the stock market."

Because Joe was working with a stockbroker, the advisor recommended a kind of annuity called a variable annuity. With the purchase of something called an income rider, Joe could get a guaranteed growth rate of 7 percent, but he didn't quite understand the fee structure or limitations of the investment he was in. All he understood was that he was getting a guaranteed growth rate of 7 percent. What's not to like about that?

Several years went by, and then Joe retired. He had met his goal of saving $1 million and felt pretty good about his prospects. Then he started noticing that the actual account balance on his variable annuity was starting to drop. At first, he thought it was due to his income payout, but the numbers weren't quite adding up. After a while, Joe started to get concerned. If he had a guaranteed 7-percent growth rate, why wasn't his account balance higher?

He went in to see a fiduciary professional who took the time to explain to him how variable annuities worked. When the professional was done peeling back all the layers of the onion, Joe got a very bad feeling. He realized that in exchange for his 7-percent guaranteed growth rate, he had paid out more money in fees during the last 10 years than what the investment was able to earn.

VARIABLE ANNUITIES: Of all the popular types of market-based investments, variable annuities continue to be among the most vexing. In our experience, most people get into these vehicles under the misguided belief that they are protecting their nest egg and preserving their retirement, without realizing that they are still in a market-based investment. If there is only one thing you learn about variable annuities, it should be this: *they CAN lose money, even if you pay extra for the guarantees.* And by lose money, we mean to the stock market. That's why they have the word variable in their name.

If you can't wait to learn "All About Annuities," check out Chapter Four. Not all annuities are market-based. The variable annuity is special in this respect. It is one type of annuity that attempts to give you the horsepower of mutual funds packaged under the durable hood of a minivan, so to speak. If you're looking for growth and safety, a variable annuity is a kind of one-size-fits-all answer that comes with a rather expensive price tag. They are much more complex than mutual funds because they are trying to give you a layer of protection and access to dependable income. They are also, generally speaking, the most expensive kind of annuity that you can own.

Just how expensive? A Morningstar 2012 report found the average fees for a variable annuity to total 2.35 percent, but if you add the living benefit rider, which is what Joe in our story above got in order to get his guaranteed

7 percent, then the average cost becomes 3.4 percent.[5] Your fees might be higher due to the individual subaccounts charged by the mutual funds inside the annuity. There are several costs associated with variable annuities:

A possible upfront sales charge, which can be similar to the front-load fees charged by Class A mutual funds

- A sliding-scale surrender charge that generally ranges anywhere from 0 to 10 percent, and which may decrease the longer you own the annuity
- Insurance charges known as the **mortality and expense risk (M&E)**, in addition to administrative costs and possible distribution charges
- Management and/or administration fees
- Underlying fund expense ratios, similar to those charged by mutual funds
- The additional expense of the rider if you want to get a guarantee
- An annual contract or maintenance charge assessed by the company that sells the annuity

---

[5] http://corporate.morningstar.com/us/documents/NASDCompliance/ADV_AIR_SubmittedReport_SideBySideComparison.pdf

With all these fees, you might wonder why anybody ever buys them. In most cases, we find that people who purchased them did so because they thought they were getting a shiny racecar that could give them a guaranteed rate of return somewhere in the neighborhood of 6 or 7 percent, like Joe in our story above. They don't realize that: 1) this type of investment can lose money during a stock market downturn even with the guaranteed protection in place, 2) the fees really add up, and 3) you have very limited access to your money. And here's the real gotcha: you still have to pay those fees even if your account takes a hit and is losing money.

Commodities: A commodity is a physical good such as oil or gold or coffee that is used in commerce and can be interchangeable with other commodities of the same kind. There are many ways to invest in commodities, but there are only four categories:

- Agriculture (corn, sugar, wheat)
- Livestock (live cattle)
- Metals (silver, gold, copper)
- Energy (crude oil, gasoline, heating oil)

The catch: you want to be aware that just because you can sell a commodity doesn't mean that you will be able to capture your just rewards at the going market price. It's helpful to think of it as similar to the buying and selling of cars. There's usually a salesman involved who offers to buy the car/gold for the *least* amount possible in hopes of marking up the car/gold and selling at a *bigger* profit for themselves, not you.

GOTCHA: While **real estate investment trusts (REITs)** are becoming more prevalent, most people are surprised to find out how **illiquid** they are, with a high potential for volatility. Many of them also include internal fees and expenses that should be understood by the investor. If you have REITs in your portfolio, mark these with a red flag in your mind and have them evaluated by a fiduciary professional.

Digital Currency: This is one investment that didn't even exist during the days our grandparents were investing, and some would even argue that it doesn't really exist now. Also known as cryptocurrency or electronic currency,

Liquidity is the ability of an investment to convert easily to cash.

with names such as Bitcoin (BTC), Litecoin (LTC), and Ethereum (ETH), digital currency is highly volatile, all the rage, and worth only what other people are willing to pay for it. It exists purely in electronic form as a money balance recorded on a stored-value card or other device. For all of human history, our currency has held or stored some sort of inherent value that consumers could use for trade. According to the Internal Revenue Service, virtual currency is a digital representation of value that functions as a medium of exchange, and so in 2014, it announced that it would treat Bitcoin as *property* rather than *currency* for tax purposes.[6] In that sense, digital currency functions more like a commodity than an actual currency. While these currencies are already trading on the futures market and likely here to stay, it's uncertain how the government will regulate them. This is a speculative and dangerous investment, in our opinion—one that is still a work in-progress, and should therefore be approached like you might the craps table at the casinos in Vegas, particularly for those investors at or nearing the time of retirement.

---

[6] https://www.irs.gov/pub/irs-drop/n-14-21.pdf

KNOW YOUR RISK NUMBER

We find that when it comes to investments, there are generally two types of investors. Both types can best be explained by thinking in terms of a clock: some people only need to know how to tell the time; other people need to know exactly how the clock works. For the engineers among you, we're going to take a deeper dive into the subject of risk and asset allocation later on in Chapter Five, when we talk about the differences between active, passive, and tactical management. But for the rest of you, here's a simplified way to think about risk:

You know those mattress commercials where one spouse is sleeping comfortably and the other one is rustling around, miserable? Consumers are encouraged to "know your sleep number" so that everyone can get a restful night's sleep. It can also be helpful to think of risk in terms of what would allow you to sleep best at night. To that end, we advise investors to "know your risk number," so to speak.

One way to identify your risk number is a rule of thumb known as the Rule of 100. The rule states that your current age subtracted from 100 should equal the percentage of your portfolio that you have allocated to market-based investments. For example, if you are 62 years old, then you should have 38 percent of your portfolio allocated to market-based investments.

100 - YOUR AGE = YOUR RISK NUMBER

Now this is by no means a hard-and-fast rule; it's just a starting point to help you understand your risk tolerance. Had Jerry in our story at the beginning of the chapter identified his risk number before retiring, he might have moved a percentage of his portfolio to safety and kept more of his money. You might also ask yourself this: if you woke up tomorrow and the balance of your investment portfolio had dropped by 73 percent, how would you feel? If the feeling isn't good, use the Rule of 100, find your risk number, and ask the question again. Using our earlier example, if only 38 percent of your portfolio (rather than 100 percent) dropped by 73 percent, how would you feel then? If you know that the remaining 62 percent is safe and enough to cover your income expenses, then maybe you're comfortable with that. If you still feel bad about it, adjust the numbers and fiddle with the dial until you can sleep at night.

Investor Checklist

Do these three things:

✓ Understand what you own.
✓ Know the goal of each investment.
✓ Identify your risk number.

CHAPTER TWO:
MUTUAL FUNDS

THE INVESTMENTS BEHIND THE CURTAIN

"Often, when investors focus too much on past performance, a fund's name or hype, they pay too little attention to how management, sales, and other costs can impact their investment over time."
~ Arthur Levitt, 25th and longest-serving Chairman of the SEC

A large percentage of the clients who come through our door invest in mutual funds, mainly because most people believe they are the only game in town. According to the Investment Company Institute, 55 million U.S. households own mutual funds, and these households represent all age groups, income levels, and educational backgrounds.[7] If you're reading this chapter, you're likely among those 55 million. Mutual funds are a popular and easy way to boost your retirement savings, and a lot

---

[7] https://www.ici.org/viewpoints/view_17_household_fund_investing

of people look to them as an immediate way to achieve diversification.

Don't get us wrong—diversification is a great story to tell, but when it comes to mutual funds, it's an incomplete story. Having mutual funds alone doesn't mean that you'll experience mitigated risk or stronger returns, no matter how wonderful your mutual funds are purported to be. There's more to the mutual fund story than typically meets the investor's eye, which is why we're pulling back the curtain, so to speak, because here's the catch: when it comes to mutual funds, it's what you *don't* know that can hurt you.

STARSTRUCK OR DUMB LUCK?

The SEC requires all funds to remind investors of this salient fact: **a fund's past performance does not necessarily predict future results.** Yet investors continue to be wooed by the allure of top-performing funds. They make their choices based on a fund's name and the hype generated by past performance, thinking something along the lines of, *If the fund is a top performer now, imagine what it can do in the future.* Why wouldn't you want to get in on it? After all, doesn't a good racehorse always come in ahead of the pack?

Have you ever heard the expression "beware the story that pleases you most"?

Strategists have looked closely at the correlation between past performance and current results, and found that from the buy-and-hold standpoint, you might actually fare better if you flip a coin when making your choices.[8] More often than not, mutual funds that are hot one year are just as likely to underperform the next. According to the S&P Persistence Scorecard, relatively few top-performing funds can consistently stay at the top, especially if you look at performance over a five-year period. The 2016 study evaluated the 641 domestic equity funds that were in the top 25 percent as of March 2014, and after a five-year period, only 0.78 percent of large-cap funds and NO mid- or small-cap funds managed to remain in the top quartile. Even after two years, only 7.33 percent of top-performing funds were still in the top quartile.[9] The moral of the story: good today doesn't equal good

---

[8] https://www.nytimes.com/2015/03/15/your-money/how-many-mutual-funds-routinely-rout-the-market-zero.html

[9] http://www.spindices.com/documents/spiva/persistence-score-card-august-2016.pdf

tomorrow, which means if you're paying premium fees under the misguided promise of premium results, you might want to put your money on a horse of a different color.

Investor Q&A: *Can my mutual fund manager sell all my shares when he knows the fund is tanking?* Specific language in the fund prospectus typically requires that the fund invest at least 80 percent of its assets in the type of investments implied by the fund name. This means that even if your broker or fund manager knows that your portfolio will lose money, and even if he or she could sell your shares and go to cash, they are legally prohibited from doing so. To get that kind of portfolio management, you need to work with a fiduciary professional who takes a tactical approach to money management.

AHEAD OF THE CLASS OR FALLING BEHIND?

We all learned in grade school that there's safety in numbers, and this is the basic premise of the mutual fund. One mutual fund will commonly contain 90 to 200 companies, the theory being that the overachievers will balance out the underperformers, and if one company goes bankrupt, it won't hurt the totality of the portfolio.

If you're choosing your mutual funds based on performance, however, you're likely not getting a realistic picture of how much you're actually going to earn. **Fund literature and marketing press generally report on a fund's performance *without* adjusting for the full impact of the operating expenses and sales charges.** Investors should be aware that shareholder fees (which are transactional sales charges or loads paid to your broker or financial advisor) are not typically included in the list of a fund's annual operating expenses. The operating expenses are ongoing and paid by you each year as a percentage of the value of your investment.

Here is a breakdown of the ongoing and transaction fees you can expect to pay inside of your mutual fund:

- **Shareholder Fees:** These are transactional fees paid directly from your investment. Sales charges or loads are paid by you as a percentage of either: 1) the offering price or 2) the lesser of the original purchase price or redemption proceeds. A front-load charge is paid at the time of purchase; a deferred sales charge, or back-load, is paid at the time of redemption.

- **Annual Operating Expenses:** These are ongoing fees based on a percentage amount of the value of your investment, paid each year that you own the investment. These fees can be broken down as follows:
    - Management fees, paid to the company that manages the fund
    - 12b-1 fees, paid for distribution and marketing (This is how the company pays for their commercials. Isn't it nice that you get to fund their advertising campaigns?)
    - Other expenses
    - Acquired fund fees and expenses

Arthur has $100,000 invested in a Class A mutual fund. The shareholder fee charges him a 5.75-percent front-load to get into the fund, but no back-load to get out of the fund. The management fee is 0.56 percent, the 12b-1 fee is 0.25 percent, other expenses are listed in the prospectus as 0.27 percent, and the acquired fund fees and expenses are 0.01 percent. The first year Arthur invests in the fund, these fees cost him $6,840. Does he see any market gains that year? Unfortunately, *no. His fund earns 6.25 percent, but he needs to earn 7 percent before he can start turning a profit. Because he is making regular contributions to his 401(k) plan and his account is growing, Arthur doesn't realize this.*

> **GOTCHA**: Beware of funds with a high **turnover rate**. Management fees can fluctuate and oftentimes the amount of portfolio turnover in a fund will have the effect of raising and/or lowering those management fees depending on the turnover rate. This can result in a drag on fund performance. Check the prospectus or ask a fiduciary to review your fund's turnover rate.

In order to disclose the cost of their fees, companies send investors something called a fund prospectus, which makes for some pretty great reading. (Not.) We actually find that most people would rather the company credit the money back to their account than spend it on printing something that they and most people

A turnover rate (or turnover ratio) is the number used to tell you how many times the holdings in a mutual fund have been changed.

will never read. (Prospectus printing costs are typically funded by the 12b-1 fees.)[10] Still, you should be aware of what you're paying and why, so let's take a look into the fee structure of mutual funds.

If you open the front page of your prospectus, you'll notice a lot of letters that might seem at first familiar. During our school days, most of us tried to get good grades, and an A was better than a B just as a B was better than a C. In the world of mutual funds, however, an A fund isn't necessarily telling you that's the best fund out there; it's telling you how the broker is compensated and what's happening on the inside in terms of fees.

Consider the following:

- **Class A Shares**: These are quite possibly the most common class of mutual funds sold. They have a sales charge or **load** that is charged upfront, when you make the investment. This is the commission paid out to your broker or fund manager, and it immediately reduces your initial investment. For example,

A load is a fee investors pay to purchase or sell a specific investment.

[10] https://www.sec.gov/fast-answers/answers12b-1feeshtm.html

if you invest $100,000 in a Class A mutual fund with a front-load fee of 5.75 percent, then your broker would get $5,750, and your investment in the fund would be $94,250. Class A shares typically offer investors breakpoints or thresholds that, once reached, reduce the sales load by a fraction of a percent. The 12b-1 fees of a Class A share are also typically lower than those of Class B and C shares.

- **Class B Shares:** You might say that B stands for back-load. Class B funds do not charge a front-load sales charge; however, they charge higher expenses than Class A shares for a period of (typically) four to eight years.[11] They also impose a **contingent deferred sales charge (CDSC)** or back-load fee if you want to get out of the fund. This is not the same thing as a redemption fee, charged by some mutual funds. For example, if you sell your shares early— typically before a period of six years— the broker or financial advisor will take a parting gift from you in the form of a fee

---

[11] http://www.finra.org/investors/alerts/class-b-mutual-fund-shares-do-they-make-grade

that will cost you anywhere from 1 to 5 percent.

> **GOTCHA**: The SEC warns investors to be cautious when the total dollars (the trade plus assets already managed by that family) being invested in a particular Class B fund exceeds $100,000. Some investors may be advised to move in and out of Class B funds when it would actually be more cost-effective to purchase a different class of shares.

- **Class C Shares:** These shares typically do not charge a front-end sales charge, so all your money starts earning for you right away. The back-load fee or CDSC is normally lower than that of Class B funds and may be eliminated after one year; however, Class C generally imposes higher annual operating expenses, primarily due to the higher 12b-1 fee. Why should the owners of Class C shares have to pay more for the marketing and distribution of the mutual fund?

We don't have an answer for you. This type of fund might be less expensive for a shorter-term investment goal because there are no front-loads and typically a lower CDSC, but for the long-term, the higher operating expenses can make this one of the most expensive investment classes that you can own.

Otto was on the golf course when he got a phone call from his broker: "Hey Otto, I'm thinking of taking you out of biotech and putting you into emerging markets. Is that okay?" Otto replied, "You're the advisor—why are you asking me?" The broker got permission to make the switch and earned himself a nice 1-percent commission fee on a $750,000 account. Otto went back to his golf game and remained oblivious. This continued for the course of 20 years, during which time Otto paid over $74,000 in operating expenses and $115,000 in switching fees when he didn't have to because he was in a mutual fund that didn't fit his long-term investment goals.

A NOTE ABOUT WORKING WITH A FIDUCIARY PROFESSIONAL

We all know the saying "it takes money to make money." But how do you know when you're paying too much for the privilege of making money? This is where the question of suitability versus fiduciary standards comes into play. We will be spending an entire chapter on the importance of choosing the right person to help you with your money decisions, but the phrase "fiduciary professional" has already come up a few times, so let's define terms:

Fiduciary Standard: financial professionals held to this standard are required by law to put their client's interests above their own. The definition as established by the Investment Advisers Act of 1940 specifically defines the fiduciary standard as consisting of duty, loyalty, and care. What does that mean? A fiduciary professional is legally prohibited from calling up his client and convincing him to switch or trade funds just because it would result in a higher commission for them. Fiduciaries adhere to the "best execution" standard, which means that when they trade securities such as mutual funds, they do so with the goal of getting the lowest-cost fees for the most efficient management of their client's portfolio.

Suitability Standards: financial professionals held to this standard are not required to place their own interests below those of the client. They only have to reasonably believe that their recommendations are suitable. Broker-dealers are held to suitability standards, and so their loyalty and duty is to the broker-dealer (the entity or bank) and not necessarily to the client they are serving.

Spend some time thinking about this and ask yourself, what standard do you want the professional handling your money to be held to?

Key Points to Remember:

- Mutual funds are not guaranteed or insured by the FDIC or any other government agency, even if you purchase them through a bank and the fund carries the bank's name.[12]

- You will pay the sales charges, annual fees, management fees and other expenses associated with your mutual funds regardless of how the funds perform. Investors may also have to pay taxes on any capital gains distribution they receive.

- Despite what your financial professional may tell you, past performance is not a reliable indicator of future performance, and you can lose money investing in mutual funds.

- All mutual funds have costs and these fees lower your returns. To find out if you can do better, shop around and compare fees by working with an independent financial professional who serves as your fiduciary.

---

[12] https://www.sec.gov/reportspubs/investor-publications/investor-pubsinwsmfhtm.html

Investor Checklist:

Do these three things:

✓ Before choosing a mutual fund based on its performance history, take a look at the fund's management, sales, and other costs.

✓ Know what fees you are paying and why. Ask yourself, are you getting what you paid for?

✓ Shop around and compare to find out if you can get the same results or better by using funds with lower fees. Better yet, work with a fiduciary professional who can shop around with your best interests in mind.

CHAPTER THREE: BANK INVESTMENTS

ARE YOU GOING BROKE SAFELY?

"Your assumptions are your windows on the world. Scrub them off every once in a while, or the light won't come in."
~ Isaac Asimov

It's been our experience that everyone is a long-term investor until they experience short-term losses. Then, they make the rush to safety. Are you guilty of this?

Most people assume that banks are the safest place for their money to be, but all investments involve some degree of risk. Believe it or not, it's possible for your money to earn returns that are so dismal, you end up doing what we in the industry call "going broke safely." If you have an amount of money that you know you need to rely on at some point during retirement, then you'll no doubt want to seek some guarantees when designing your retirement plan. This chapter will help shed some light on why you might not want to limit yourself to bank investments alone, and how understanding the tradeoff between liquidity, safety, and return can help prevent you from making foolish mistakes.

WHY DO PEOPLE INVEST IN BANKS?

As established brick-and-mortar entities, banks have a long history of being the place where you can safely stash your cash. It's comforting to walk through the glass doors of your financial institution and see the logo that affirms: FDIC-insured. That guarantee helps investors to sleep well at night because they know that even if a Jessie James wannabe were to rob the bank tomorrow, they can make you whole again, reimbursing you for up to $250,000. While banks are not legally required to have FDIC insurance, most banks do because they know their customers value the security.

Another reason people like banks is because they're convenient. You can pull up to a drive-through window or a bank-operated ATM, or even interact online to complete mortgage payments, make deposits, or line your wallet with cold hard cash. What's not to like about that?

Banks make it easy to access your money,

which makes them a good place to keep an emergency fund. But is it a safe place to store large amounts of money that you know you need to rely on for retirement?

The third and most unfortunate reason why people invest in banks is because they don't realize that other alternatives exist. Currently, the rates on bank CDs are so low that many people jokingly call them "certificates of disappoint," and while this is a funny thing to say, it's not funny when your savings accounts end up being too depleted to carry you through retirement.

Investor Q&A: *Is my credit union FDIC-insured?* Credit unions aren't typically insured by the FDIC, but they offer consumers the same kind of insurance through the National Credit Union Administration (NCUA). This insurance operates much like FDIC insurance, guaranteeing depositors up to $250,000.

THIS ISN'T YOUR GRANDFATHER'S RETIREMENT

How many of you reading this remember the days when bank CDs were paying out double-digit returns as high as 12 percent? Back in the late '70s and early '80s, investors could get the safety of bank CDs with some pretty respectable returns, and those who were retired with a pension and Social Security never even had to mess with the stock market. Sadly, the rates on bank CDs reached their peak in 1984, and bank rates historically speaking are lower than the rate of **inflation**.[13] We call earning rates that low "being paid in gumballs" and believe that you can and should do better.

While it's true that the Federal Reserve is trying to normalize rates, yearning for the good ol' days isn't a good strategy if you're retiring anytime soon. Bank rates are directly tied to inflation, so when they're earning double-digits, that means inflation is running rampant. Sure, you might be earning decent returns from the bank, but how much will it cost to fill your tank with gas and your cupboards with food?

If the money you have in long-term savings accounts isn't at least earning enough to keep up with inflation, then the purchasing power of your dollars gradually erodes. It's a lot like

Inflation is the general rate at which the price of goods and services gradually rises

---

[13] https://www.bankrate.com/banking/cds/you-earned-how-much-a-brief-history-of-cd-rates/#slide=1

building your dream house right on the edge of a riverbank: over time, the ground beneath you may start to crumble, you could lose footing, and you risk having your house swept away along with everything in it. While this might sound a bit dramatic, keep in mind that inflation coincides with tax erosion. If the money you invest in the bank is non-qualified, then the interest earned by your CDs will also be taxed at normal income rates. Not only will you be earning less than inflation, but you'll also be paying Uncle Sam for the privilege, which is why relying too heavily on bank investments can actually cost you money.

MARKET
ADVISORY GROUP

Banks - CD's

$100,000 Initial Investment

CD Rate (10 Yrs.)	2.16%	$2160
Inflation Rate (10 Yrs.)	2.42%	-$2420
Taxes	15% Federal 8.5% State	-$507
Effective End of the Year Acount Value	$99,233	

DO YOU HAVE A FOOLISH FUND?

Banks are an appropriate place to keep some extra money on hand in the event of an emergency, but unless you're doing it correctly, your emergency fund can easily become a foolish fund. There are two ways this can happen:

1. Too much money sitting in the bank: You don't want to be giving away the potential to earn money on returns. While it's true that you need to have a sizable sum come retirement, you certainly won't be spending ALL of that money right away. What you don't need to spend this year or in the next five or 10 years has the potential to grow for you, like a crockpot on a low simmer. If you choose to keep too much of it someplace where it's not even keeping up with inflation, then you have what we call "lazy money."

2. Not enough money sitting in the bank: You also don't want to have your emergency money someplace where spending it could mean taking a loss. Relying on volatile investments such as stocks, bonds, or mutual funds as your source of backup cash could mean that you end up liquidating when the market is low;

furthermore, if this is qualified money, then you'll also incur a tax obligation.

CREATING A COMPREHENSIVE RETIREMENT PLAN

It's basically foolish to set yourself up so that you have to pay for the privilege of accessing your own money. When you take the time to create a comprehensive retirement plan, investments are chosen with several goals in mind. Obviously, you don't want to run out of money. How you allocate your resources to certain investments will allow you to achieve the greatest efficiency with the maximum returns and lowest fees. Furthermore, all the parts of the plan should work together so that you don't incur unnecessary taxes or hardship should an emergency arise.

A sudden need for extra cash can be a happy event: maybe your daughter is getting married or you found your dream cottage or you want to send your grandson to Harvard. Whatever the reason, the job of a good financial professional is to help you design a plan that works for you, not against you.

How much should you keep on hand in an emergency fund? Experts typically suggest that you keep three to six months' worth of expenses in the bank where you can have access to the funds within 24 hours. However, if you build a retirement plan correctly, then you'll have a balance of safety, liquidity, and return built right into your plan. Our clients, for example, know that they are normally two or three business days away from having access to cash funds.

Why are safety, liquidity, and return important components of an income plan?

- **Safety**: the guaranteed return of your principal
- **Liquidity**: the ability of an investment to convert easily to cash
- **Return**: a measure of profit earned by your money

Typically, any single investment that you chose for your retirement portfolio will do a good job of giving you access to two of these three elements, but it won't do so hot in the third area.

For example, stocks have the potential for great returns. Since they are traded and sold daily, you can have access to your money within three to six business days should you decide to sell. As a market-based investment, however, stocks are not considered safe because they do not guarantee the return of your principal.

On the other hand, bank investments such as CDs can give you a guarantee on the return of your principal in addition to a guaranteed fixed rate of return at maturity. In terms of liquidity, however, if you want to get a rate that is higher than 1 percent, you typically have to tie up your money for a period of years. You can find bank CDs for one, three, or six months, or one to five years, but generally, the sooner you need your money back, the lower the fixed rate will be.

Learning how to evaluate your investments in terms of safety, liquidity, and return will help you to better balance your portfolio so that you can prevent the unnecessary erosion of your money. It can also prevent the foolishness of having to pay to access your own cash. Comprehensive plans are living, breathing things with allocations that aren't set in stone. They can and should change with you as you go along because hopefully, you'll be retired for quite a long time.

Investor Checklist:

Do these three things:

✓ Protect the money you need for income by evaluating your allocations in terms of safety, liquidity, and return.

✓ Keep an appropriate amount of emergency cash reserves in a money market or savings account.

✓ Adjust accordingly.

CHAPTER FOUR:
ALL ABOUT ANNUITIES

BECAUSE THE MARKET GOES UP UNTIL IT DOESN'T

"Don't fall in love with your investments; fall in love with the results."

~ Market Advisory Group

Every Wednesday Paul would walk three blocks to the corner coffee shop, where he would meet with Frank and Otto to talk about the retired life. They kept up with one another, where they were traveling with their wives, and what kinds of activities the grandkids were involved in. They also talked about their investments from time to time, particularly during 2008 when the market crashed.

One day Paul sat down with his coffee and realized the conversation had turned to who was hiring senior citizens and what kind of hours they could get.

"What are you guys talking about?" said Paul. "Going back to work?"

"Well, yeah," said Otto. "I'm losing money like crazy."

"Why?"

"Haven't you seen what the market is doing?" Frank chimed in.

"It doesn't matter what the market is doing," said Paul. "I'm in annuities. I'm still getting paid."

They both scratched their heads and looked at him.

"Your money isn't in the market?"

"Not the money I need for my income."

Walking back home that day, Paul felt pretty good. He never did lose any money during 2008 because he didn't have to sell when the market was at record lows. He and his wife took a cruise to Greece where they explored the ancient wonders of the world.

Love 'em or hate 'em, there's nothing that can do what an annuity can do: it's the only type of investment vehicle that takes a sum of money and turns it into a guaranteed stream of income. This is what corporations used to create the beloved pensions of yesteryear, and it's the basis of the Social Security program we still use today. In fact, annuities have many of the same benefits and features as Social Security:

- The benefit payment can be set to last as long as the life of an individual, no matter how long that individual lives.
- The benefit can grow at a guaranteed rate of return.
- The longer you wait to tap into it, the more the money may grow to achieve a higher amount of income.

Annuities also have the option for some benefits that Social Security does NOT have:

- An annuity can be paid out to a spouse in the event of an individual's death.
- You can add money to an annuity to increase the potential for income return.
- You can request that any money left in your annuity be transferred to your beneficiaries so that the money stays in your family.

If annuities can do all this, then why do so many people hate them?

It was Ted Rubin who said, "A brand is what a business does, a reputation is what people remember." Not all annuities can do the same thing, and those that have a bad reputation are the ones that tend to stick most in people's minds. Yet in spite of all the talk about annuities, very few people really understand what they do. This chapter is here to change that.

GOTCHA: The most commonly-held license in the financial realm is the kind held by an annuity salesperson. If he or she can ONLY sell you annuities, then guess what they'll recommend for you? Annuities are not right for everyone and they are seldom right for 100 percent of your portfolio.

Investor Q&A: *Is my annuity FDIC-insured?* Because annuities are life insurance products, they are backed by the claims-paying ability of the life insurance company. Investors are taught to investigate the financial strength of the company, but this can be somewhat vexing because each of the five different agencies that rate the financial strength of insurance companies has its own rating scales and standards. You may not want to rely on what the insurance company says about their ratings because they're likely to highlight a higher rating from one agency and ignore a lower rating from another agency.[14]

---

[14] https://www.iii.org/article/how-to-assess-the-financial-strength-of-an-insurance-company

THE THREE BIG PLAYERS

An annuity is a type of life insurance contract whereby the investor exchanges a sum of money for an income payment that is set to begin either immediately or later. It if begins later, the account balance may grow at a guaranteed rate for a set period of time. Some annuities also have added features such as long-term care benefits, or they can be structured specifically to grow money for your beneficiaries. On the downside, annuities are often sold by professionals who stand to earn a rather high commission from selling them, so they might unduly influence the investor. This can make it difficult for the consumer to figure out if an annuity is really in their best interest.

In terms of *liquidity, safety, and return,* annuities are generally an **illiquid** asset with strong elements of safety and the potential for return. There are some types of annuities that can give you a guarantee on the return of your principal and protection against the downside of the market; other types of annuities offer the possibility of either direct or indirect market returns. In terms of liquidity, deferred annuities

Illiquid refers to the state of an asset that can't be easily or quickly sold for conversion to cash without a loss in value.

are typically a long-term investment that can tie up your money for a period of years, during which time you may typically only access up to 10 percent of your principal annually. To access more than that, you may have to pay a penalty.

In the annuity world, we have three main types of deferred annuities with three rather distinct personalities:

#1 The Fixed Annuity: You might think of the fixed annuity as the nice old lady who lives next door. It gives you a fixed rate of return for a fixed number of years, usually anywhere from one to five years. After that period of time is over, the insurance company will declare the interest rate again. Its biggest strength is its safety: there is no possibility of loss due to the market. Its biggest downside is that your returns are limited to whatever interest rate the company declares, and that rate is set for a number of years, which means that if interest rates go up, you're stuck with something lower that you can't get out of without penalty for a certain period of time.

#2 The Variable Annuity: You might think of the variable annuity as the "everyone eats before you do" annuity. When you're in this type of annuity, you become like the good host who defers to her guests so that everybody has plenty to eat before she even picks up your plate. This is one party you might not want to throw. We talked earlier in Chapter One about how this market-based investment is layered with fees. The variable annuity is the only annuity that is said to be a market-based investment. It can typically give you more horsepower than the fixed or indexed annuity because its interest rate is tied to the underlying mutual funds, but you do have to pay for this. To manage the volatility, the insurance company transfers the cost of that market risk onto you by charging more fees. Even if you pay extra for the contractual guarantees, please be advised that in a variable annuity, the value of your actual account can still fall and you can lose money due to market performance. Many investors through no fault of their own mistakenly believe that they are getting a guaranteed rate of return on the growth of their principal when really, they're getting a rate lock on a "fake" money account used by the insurance company to calculate the income payment. We've seen cases with variable annuities where it took as long as 18 years before the investor started earning anything above the cost of their fees.

#3 The Fixed-Indexed Annuity: You might describe the growing popularity of the fixed-indexed annuity as the "I'll have whatever he's having" annuity. This is an indexed hybrid that offers investors aspects of the variable annuity built on the chassis of a fixed vehicle. It has principal guarantees similar to the fixed annuity, but it also has more choices for growth. With an indexed annuity, you have the option of choosing to allocate your future potential growth to a market index such as the NASDAQ or the S&P 500. If the index goes up, you get a share of the gains; if the index goes down or sideways, the insurance company will not give you a negative return, nor will the value of your actual account fall. Furthermore, once they credit those returns to your account, they become locked-in so your principal isn't affected by negative market growth. This makes it an attractive growth vehicle for the money you know you need to rely on for income. Depending on how it's structured, you may also have access to your money. One criticism of the indexed annuity is its complexity, which is why you want to work with an advisor who takes the time to explain how these investment vehicles work.

Investor Q&A: *I thought an annuity never gave you access to your money?* There is one type of annuity that functions most like traditional pensions. Single premium immediate annuities (SPIAs) are typically annuitized. This means that an investor gives up control of their cash in exchange for a consistent (and immediate) stream of income.

GOTCHA: Beware of the annuity salesperson who touts tax deferral as the reason you should roll over your IRA or 401(k) into a variable annuity. By definition, those retirement accounts are already receiving tax-deferred growth, so there is no additional benefit to you, the investor, although there may be a high commission for the advisor.

Ron and Kirstin were ages 57 and 55 respectively when they started wondering if there wasn't something they should be doing to better position their assets. They had multiple accounts, and although they had already worked with their broker to secure their retirement income, they noticed they were paying a lot of fees, and they weren't sure they had gotten the right kind of annuity.

They made an appointment with a fiduciary professional to have their portfolio analyzed for efficiency and risk. The fiduciary asked them, "How much of this money do you never want to lose?" They answered, "We know we want to protect 80 percent of this money." Then the advisor gave them the news: "Do you realize that currently, only 30 percent of your portfolio is protected?" 70 percent of their $1.3 million retirement fund was directly exposed to stock market risk. Ron and Kirstin did not realize that.

The advisor also found several instances where they were paying much more in fees than necessary. They had $387,000 in an Edward Jones Mutual Funds account invested in Class C shares that cost them an annual, ongoing fee of 1.85 percent. In a Wells Fargo brokerage account, they had $692,000 with an ongoing fee of 3.75 percent. They had also invested $250,000 in a variable annuity with an annual fee of 3.25 percent. The cost just to run the portfolio totaled $38,109 a year. Ron and Kirstin had no idea they were paying that much in fees.

After working with a fiduciary, they were able to get better income guarantees with more *options for liquidity using an indexed annuity with an income rider for an annual fee of 1.05 percent. They also got a professionally-managed investment account for their growth needs. After they reallocated, their new annual portfolio cost was only $17,731. Ron and Kirstin were able to save $20,378 annually in fees, and they also reduced their risk, exposing only 20 percent of their assets while protecting the other 80 percent.*

Now, Ron and Kirstin are sleeping much better at night.

THE BIG BAD WOLF

We all know the story of the big bad wolf: he huffs, and puffs, and blows your house down. If your retirement income is made of sticks—i.e., heavily allocated in market-based investments with high or unnecessary fees—then when the wolf of a market downturn blows, your retirement accounts are also likely to fall down.

During the writing of this book, the stock market took its biggest drop since 2011: the Dow Jones Industrial Average tumbled in a single day by 1,175 points, by far its worst closing point decline on record.[15] We are also entering into what many experts claim to be a bear market for bonds.[16]   Too many advisors today use market-based investments to mitigate risk for their clients' portfolios, relying on mutual funds or single stocks or laddered bond portfolios. With these strategies, investors who are on a fixed income could be facing a future income crisis.

We advocate for a "protect first, grow second" approach. Why would you want to jeopardize your nest egg when it's reached its highest point? While many people jump to the conclusion that a "protect first, grow second" philosophy means they won't get a rate of return, ask yourself, why take on risk and not get paid for it, especially on the money that you know you need for your retirement income?

Annuities offer the investor the opportunity to shelter a portion of their portfolio using guaranteed strategies that can typically keep up with or do better than the average annual rate of inflation. They can also give you a guaranteed income stream set for a period of time that you choose: five years, 10 years, or life, for either yourself or you and your spouse. With these kinds of guarantees, investors get

---

[16] https://www.bloomberg.com/news/articles/2018.../this-bond-market-could-get-uglier

what we call a SWAN retirement plan: Sleep Well At Night.

The choice, of course, is completely up to you.

Investor Checklist:

Do these three things:

✓ Open up your mind and forget everything you think you know about annuities.

✓ Identify which kind of annuity fits your needs.

✓ Protect first, grow second.

CHAPTER FIVE:
IS YOUR PORTFOLIO WEARING A FANNY PACK?

MONEY MANAGEMENT STYLES

"We cannot direct the wind, but we can adjust the sails."
~ Dolly Parton

Nobody wants to be the fuddy-duddy wearing the outdated outfit at the party. Investments also have trends and seasons and hot picks, but it can sometimes be difficult to figure out what's a good fit. Sometimes popular products or new stocks get a lot of hype, while the classics are overlooked; other times there's nothing really new at all, just a lot of smoke and mirrors and salespeople making noise.

The consequences of making a fashion faux pas don't extend very far past a bruised ego; an allocation mistake, however, can have far-reaching and devastating consequences, particularly for the investor who is at or near the time of retirement. If you're somebody who follows trends, then you might have heard the news: the 4-percent rule is no longer in. This isn't a product or investment, but a management strategy designed to give investors nearing retirement peace of mind. This chapter will guide you through what you need to know about portfolio management so that you can keep up with the times and form an opinion on which style best fits you.

WHY THE 4-PERCENT RULE IS BROKEN

The 4-percent rule was developed back in 1994 by California-based financial planner William Bengen. A graduate of MIT, Bengen came up with his rule to answer a question his clients were asking him: "How much can I safely withdraw from my portfolio over the course of a 30-year retirement?" It's a good question, and one that Bengen answered by analyzing historical return data using the year 1926 as a starting point; he examined every 30-year period thereafter up until the paper was published in 1994.[17] According to his calculations, the typical 60/40 stock-and-bond portfolio could support an annual withdrawal

---

[17] https://www.finra.org/investors/what-you-need-know-about-4-percent-rule

rate of 4 percent, adjusted annually for inflation, for a period of 30 years without running out of money.

For many years investors followed this rule. When the time of retirement neared, they met with their advisor, filled out the paperwork, and had 4 percent automatically withdrawn from their portfolio as income during retirement. This worked okay until the intermediate-term real interest rates dropped so low that they are currently about 4 percent less than their historical average.[18] We've also entered into a global economy, stocks are traded over the Internet, and news that affects market behavior travels with the push of a button. Investment conditions today are decidedly different than those used to develop Bengen's rule. If a market crash like 2008 were to happen now and you lost a large portion of your savings early in retirement, then following the 4-percent rule likely wouldn't protect you. A team of professors working with the head of retirement research at Morningstar put together a report titled "The 4% Rule Is Not Safe in a Low-Yield World." What they found was that to be safe, investors should withdraw no more than 2.8

---

[18] http://www.retirementestateplan.com/wp-content/up-loads/2015/07/the-four-percentage-rule-may-not-work.pdf

percent of their portfolio—a percentage so small that it might not satisfy the income needs of the average retiree.[19]

We'd also argue that in our experience, 4 percent isn't enough to satisfy the income needs of most people, either. Moreover, it can be dangerous to put your retirement on autopilot, no matter the amount you are withdrawing. It's often argued that for long-term goals, investors can afford to lose money because if you stay in the market long enough, you'll eventually get your money back. While this may be true, the one thing investors can't get back is time. That's why it's important to recognize when you enter into what we in the business call the "retirement red zone."

Ethan in our story below was living off what he felt to be a modest amount, automatically deducted from his accounts, because following the 4-percent rule didn't give him enough income. He needed $2,000 a month to supplement his Social Security:

Ethan retired at age 65 with $236,859.00 in his portfolio. He had $24,000 deducted annually from his account for income. During his first year

[19] http://www.retirementestateplan.com/wp-content/uploads/2015/07/the-four-percentage-rule-may-not-work.pdf

of retirement, his portfolio lost 12.31 percent and his account balance dropped to $183,701.66. Year two he saw a 20-percent loss. He still took out his income of $24,000 and his account balance dropped to $121,436. After a third year of loss, Ethan called his broker, worried about running out of money. "Stay in the market," his broker said. "It always comes back."

Ethan thought that staying in the market was the only way he could have a chance at earning his money back, so he didn't get out. Sure enough, in the following year Ethan saw a whopping 22.24-percent return and his account went up from $114,437 to $115,888. For the next five years, his account earned well and he continued to take out his income.

The year Ethan celebrated his 75th birthday, his account earned a nice 21-percent gain. His broker reported that his portfolio had averaged an 8.91-percent return over the last 10 years, and his doctor gave him a clean bill of health. None of

this news made Ethan happy. He has realized too late that he still hasn't recovered from his first few years of loss and he never will. At the age of 75, he only has $5,266 left.

ARE YOU IN THE RED ZONE?

It's easy to make money in the market when the markets are going up. So easy, in fact, that the strategies most people use for growing money encourage a kind of "set it and forget it" mentality. While this can work during your accumulation years, everything changes once you near retirement. Management strategies become much more critical because NOT losing during the market lows becomes even more important than capturing the highest of the market highs. This is a concept difficult for most investors to grasp.

To explain why loss matters more, we like to use a football analogy. When a team enters the red zone, they are in the area of the field between the 20-yard line and the goal line. This means they've gained enough yardage to be within striking distance of a touchdown. Every spectator in the stands moves to the edge of their seat because to drop the ball now would mean losing the chance to score. The fate of the entire game could be at stake.

The **retirement red zone** is when investors face very similar stakes. They are sitting within striking distance of their goal, somewhere around seven to eight years away from retirement, OR seven to eight years after crossing into retirement. This is the time when your accounts are at their most vulnerable because they've gained the most yardage, so to speak, and you have the most to lose.

Remember Jerry from our story in Chapter One? He retired with a fraction of the benefits he deserved, just like Ethan in our story above, because he lost a significant portion of his savings while in the red zone. Losing at this point damages the compounding muscle of your investment portfolio and that, combined with income withdrawals, is what can make it impossible to recover. In fact, we can take the exact same rate of return and the exact same pot of money that Ethan started out with—$236,859.00—and just by reversing the order of the gains and losses, we can give him a balance of $315,794.46 at the end of 10 years instead of $0. This kind of risk is known as the **sequence of returns**, and it's something you want to be aware of because it is completely and utterly outside of your control.

Original Principal $236,859

| | Investor A | | | Investor B | |
Age	Return	Balance	Withdrawals	Return	Balance
66	-12.31%	$183,701.66	$24,000	8.28%	$232,470.93
67	-20.83%	$121,436.60	$24,000	27.10%	$271,470.55
68	14.00%	$114,437.73	$24,000	-2.20%	$241,498.19
69	22.24%	$115,888.68	$24,000	14.70%	$252,998.43
70	9.80%	$103,245.77	$24,000	19.00%	$277,068.13
71	4.32%	$83,705.98	$24,000	32.90%	$344,223.54
72	10.90%	$68,829.94	$24,000	11.10%	$358,432.36
73	2.70%	$46,688.34	$24,000	-9.80%	$299,305.99
74	3.21%	$24,187.04	$24,000	5.30%	$291,169.20
75	21.00%	$5,266.32	$24,000	16.70%	$315,794.46
76	16.70%	**$0.00**	$24,000	21.00%	$358,111.30
77	5.30%	$0.00	$24,000	3.21%	$345,606.67
78	-9.80%	$0.00	$24,000	2.70%	$330,938.05
79	11.10%	$0.00	$24,000	10.90%	$343,010.30
80	32.90%	$0.00	$24,000	4.32%	$333,828.34
81	19.00%	$0.00	$24,000	9.80%	$342,543.52
82	14.70%	$0.00	$24,000	22.24%	$394,725.20
83	-2.20%	$0.00	$24,000	14.00%	$425,986.73
84	27.10%	$0.00	$24,000	-20.83%	$313,253.69
85	8.28%	$0.00	$24,000	-12.31%	$250,692.16
	8.91%	Average		8.91%	Average

GOTCHA: It's possible to earn a positive rate of return and still lose money. Check out this crazy math: imagine you have $100 and you average a 50-percent rate of return during year one, so you now have $150. During year two, you lose 50 percent, so your account balance is now $75. The average rate of return says you earned 0 percent, but in reality, you lost $25.

MANAGEMENT STRATEGIES 101

After spending a lifetime growing a nest egg, investors have been taught to train their eye on the rate of return. They ask their advisors, "How much money can you make me?" And they judge the performance of their portfolio based on the average annual rate of return. Unfortunately, this is hardly the only metric that matters. Instead, retrain your eye to **look at the growth of an account balance over time**—specifically, the period of time during which you'll be retired—and ask your advisor, "How much money can you save me?"

It's really not your fault if you're overly focused on the rate of return. For the past 20 or 30 years, you've been tucking away money even when it wasn't easy, and it's certainly a pleasure to watch those account balances go steadily upwards. Growth matters, before and during retirement. But what you have to keep in mind as you choose your allocations now, during the period directly before and after retirement, is that *loss matters more.*

Many investors are under the assumption that when they pay management fees to their advisor, this means there is a human being out there keeping an eye on their money. They believe this person has the ability to move them in and out of funds in a way that best meets their investment objectives and overall goals. Sadly, in most situations, what people have are passive management accounts in situations where fund managers are prohibited from moving money out even when the account is rapidly dropping.

Let's take a look at the difference between the two management strategies:

Passive Strategy: Fund managers or investors buy into funds with the hope that their value goes up over time. Buy and hold is one example of a passive investment strategy. An investor who employs this strategy holds an investment regardless of market volatility with the belief that in the long run, the market will provide a fair rate of return. This particular strategy can do well in a bull market when stocks are consistently rising. However, as stocks continue to rise, they tend to become very expensive and overvalued, which hinders the internal value of the stock and limits its upside potential.

Generally speaking, buy and hold is a hands-off approach to investing where the advisor doesn't have to think about the changes in the economic cycles. If you've ever been concerned about your money in a declining market, only to be told "not to worry about it" or "over time the market always comes back," then you may be in a passive strategy. We'd also like to point out that in our opinion, hope is not a good strategy.

Active Strategy: Also called active investing, this refers to a portfolio management style where the fund manager makes specific investments for the investor with the goal of outperforming an investment benchmark index. **Tactical asset allocation (TAA)** is one example of an active strategy. Our favored approach, it allows us to change investment holdings based on economic conditions. If we feel an investment is out of favor, we can simply sell it and deploy that capital elsewhere, or if market conditions dictate, we can go to cash. This allows us to achieve two important objectives:

- Save money
- Earn money

We seek to save money by getting out of the market before it hits its lowest lows. Preservation is a consideration we take very seriously, particularly for the investor who is in the red zone. We are not afraid to go to cash if we feel the market is overpriced or presents more risk than the potential reward.

We earn money by timing our opportunities and investing during what we believe to be a low price. Think about it: when asset prices are lower than their fundamental value, it only makes sense that they will give you higher rates of return in the long run. Conversely, when asset prices are expensive, they are overvalued. An active management strategy makes every attempt to take advantage of market volatility by simply buying low and selling high. A tactical approach involves continual risk management through portfolio rebalancing with a flexible target.

As a tactical investor, you only want to own assets that are priced within a margin of safety. Owning assets priced below their intrinsic value can potentially yield high, long-term returns and preserve capital even when risks are high.

JACK BE NIMBLE, JACK BE QUICK

As you approach the time of retirement, it's important to think about your investments in terms of your retirement timeline. To take a significant loss while in the red zone, you might not have the time to earn the money back before you have to start making withdrawals.

Think carefully about your investment goals. Now that you have accumulated a large sum of money—now that you are in the red zone—ask yourself, how much of this money do you want to keep? How much do you never, *ever* want to have a chance to lose?

When you work with a fiduciary who practices tactical management, you're able to take a more nimble approach to investing. This allows you to choose investment vehicles and allocations based on certain goals. You won't be restricted to blanket strategies or certain investments, and you won't have to "wait it out" and watch your accounts lose money during what may be a critical time in your investment timeline. As the quote by Dolly Parton suggests, we can't control the market, but we can certainly remain nimble and make adjustments. How far away are you from retirement? If the answer is 10 years or fewer, then it might be time to rethink your allocation strategy.

Investor Checklist:

Do these three things:

✓ Understand that the 4-percent rule may no longer be a safe withdrawal strategy.

✓ Consider asset preservation if you are in the retirement red zone, where losing too much money could negatively affect the long-term viability of your portfolio.

✓ Choose between active and passive investment strategies based on your investment timeline.

CHAPTER SIX:
WHAT YOU NEED TO KNOW ABOUT

THE PROFESSIONAL WHO HANDLES YOUR MONEY

"If you have more than $50,000 to invest, you should fire your broker and find an investment advisor."

~ Arthur Levitt, Former SEC Chairman[20]

It's one thing to save the money, but quite another to figure out what to do with it. It was B.J. Palmer who once said, "Knowledge is knowing a fact, wisdom is knowing what to do with that fact." If you've been with us so far, reading this book, then hopefully you've gained some general knowledge and facts about investments. That, combined with your personal investing experience, could mean you're ready to find a professional who, with their wisdom, can help you implement those facts.

---

[20] Levitt, Arthur. "Three: Analyze This." Take on the Street. Vintage, 2002. Print

But how do you find an advisor you can trust? Not all financial professionals have the same licenses and skills, and as we discussed earlier, not all of them are held to the same standards.

It also bears mentioning that just because you're already working with an advisor doesn't mean that your money is in good hands. As the quote by Arthur Levitt suggests, your financial professional may not have your best interests in mind. This chapter is here to help you figure out: *who is poised to profit more, you or your advisor?*

HOW TO HIRE A FINANCIAL PROFESSIONAL

You have a job that needs to be done: you want to allocate your resources in the best way possible to come up with a financial plan that will see you safely through retirement. This is no small job. It's not even a one-time-and-it's-done kind of job. Unlike building a house or baking a cake, a plan has to be able to change and grow with you during the 20 to 30 years that are retirement, because things in your life are going to change. You might move to a different state, sell your house, start a business, or get married. Today's investors also have to remain nimble in order to make the most of market opportunities.

Knowing all of this, imagine a room full of financial professionals. All of them are candidates who claim they can help you manage this money by getting you into the kinds of vehicles and strategies that will do the greatest good. Most people are familiar with the concept of doing an honest day's work for an honest day's pay, but the financial industry does things a little differently. They give you two choices:

1. You can pay your financial professional the equivalent of five years' worth of salary upfront, on the day that you hire them, regardless of whether they do a great job for you.

2. Or, you can hire your professional and pay a small percentage of your portfolio annually, based on how much money they are able to earn you, so that they are incentivized and tied in part to your success.

Perhaps you read over option one and

wondered, *Why would anyone do that?* There would be no guarantee that the professional would show up to work after the first year, let alone after the first day. With this system, the employer has no control whatsoever over what that employee might do, and yet, this is what millions of investors do when they choose commission-based advisors. They say, "I have so much trust in you that I'm going to pay you a salary upfront!" Now, who do you think is getting the better end of that deal?

Anyone determined enough can make an argument as to why they are the best person to manage your money. At the end of the day, however, no one will care more about this money than you do. Vet your advisor carefully by understanding the differences in qualifications, fee structures, and the standards they are held to.

FINANCIAL PROFESSIONALS:
TERMS, LICENSES, AND HOW THEY GET PAID

Licensed Insurance Professionals: This is where most financial professionals get their start, by selling insurance products. A licensed insurance agent is not just able to sell life, home, and car insurance, they can also offer you different types of annuities such as those talked about in Chapter Four. Licensed insurance agents typically receive a commission on the sale of annuity products, and if they are working under the umbrella of a certain company, they may also be limited as to which life insurance or annuities they can offer you. This could unduly influence them to recommend products that are not in your best interests (i.e., pay out a higher commission to them rather than a higher retirement income/ lower fee structure for you).

As of the writing of this book, life insurance agents are held to a suitability standard, even when they are making recommendations for IRAs or money in qualified retirement plans.[21] We mention this because the Department of Labor's fiduciary rule could change all that, and some states such as New York are imposing a best-interest standard for all professionals who work with money held in retirement plans. Regardless of what happens with the fiduciary rule, there are still those financial professionals who choose to hold themselves to the fiduciary standard.

----

[21] http://www.investmentnews.com/article/20180119/ FREE/180119908/state-fiduciary-rules-may-be-reckon- ing-for-life-insurance-industry

Investor Q&A: *Why does my broker only recommend the variable type of annuity?* A variable annuity is a market-based investment and as such, it is the type of annuity brokers most often sell. Commission, fees, and broker-dealer relationships with parent companies typically dictate what types of annuities they are allowed to offer.

Licensed Securities Agents: A financial professional with a Series 6 license has a limited-investment securities license. He or she can sell you investments that are packaged, such as mutual funds and variable annuities. A Series 7 license enables your professional to sell pretty much any type of individual market-based investment such as stocks, bonds, and variable annuities. They may not be authorized to sell commodities, real estate, or life insurance. These professionals are typically known as stockbrokers (or brokers for short), and they can collect commissions on the sale of mutual funds and stocks. (For a list of the commissions and fees a broker earns from the sale of a mutual fund, see Chapter Two.) Brokers and registered representatives are typically held to suitability standards unless the professional is working under the umbrella of an investment advisory firm. Brokers and **registered representatives** also typically work for a large company or investment firm and are said to be representatives of that company. This means they can ONLY offer you the investments sold by their company. They may not offer you investments sold by other entities unless they are acting as an independent agent.

Investor Q&A: *What does it mean if my advisor has dual registration?* A large number of financial professionals act as both investment advisors and brokers, particularly if they are working for a large company. If they recommend a fee-based account where they sell you investments such as mutual funds, then they may receive a commission, thereby functioning as your broker, in which case the lower of the two legal standards typically applies. When in doubt, ask, "Are you serving as my fiduciary?"

Licensed Investment Advisors: These are financial professionals registered with the SEC who have passed the Series 65 Uniform

Registered representatives are financial professionals who work for a brokerage company. They are called representatives because they represent the company they work for when trading investment products for their clients.

Investment Advisor Law exam. This gives them the authority to provide investment and planning advice for a fee, and they are required by most states to register or become licensed.

As an individual or business, they are known as **investment advisor representatives (IARs) or registered investment advisory firms (RIAs).** Market Advisory Group, for instance, is an RIA. These professionals may also hold other licenses so they are qualified to offer you securities or life insurance products, or Social Security and tax planning advice. Regardless of what they offer and what licenses they hold, they are always held to a fiduciary standard of duty and care.

Recommendations from a licensed investment advisor must be both suitable for your situation and in your best interests because that is the legal obligation of all RIAs and IARs. They don't represent a company, bank, or organization when they make security recommendations or give investment advice; they represent YOU, the client. Licensed investment advisors are fee-only advisors, not fee-based. This means that they do not accept commissions or sales incentives, but rather, they earn a percentage based on assets under management.

GOTCHA: Do not confuse licensed investment advisors, who are fiduciary professionals, with the more general term "financial advisor." A lot of financial professionals call themselves advisors, but only licensed investment advisors are held to the fiduciary standard of care.

WHY IT PAYS (LITERALLY) TO WORK WITH A FIDUCIARY

In August of 2013, David Blanchett and Paul Kaplan of Morningstar published a paper titled "Alpha, Beta, and Now . . . Gamma." This report examined the additional value that can be achieved by the investor who makes more intelligent and cohesive financial planning decisions. The study included the retirement income metric, tax efficiency, and liability-relative asset allocations for portfolio optimization. What they found could become key for the investor who is worried about running out of money. According to their research, coordinated investment decisions can potentially earn investors as much as 22.6 percent above the portfolio managed without coordinated decisions.[22] On a million-dollar portfolio, that translates to another $226,000. The difference-maker and the wisdom to help coordinate these decisions may be the fiduciary professional who is able to customize investment plans for the individual.

Do you remember the mattress commercials we talked about back in Chapter One? These ads depict a typical married couple where the husband is sleeping comfortably and the wife is restless and rustling around, or vice versa. The catchphrase "know your sleep number" encourages consumers to address this so that they can both get a restful night's sleep. As fiduciary professionals, we also look at retirement planning and asset allocation in terms of restful slumbers, and we have our own acronym to help investors remember what's at stake. The SWAN plan stands for:

Sleep Well At Night

There are many things to consider as you approach retirement. Your peace of mind is one of them. By choosing to work with a fiduciary,

[22] https://corporate.morningstar.com/US/documents/ResearchPa-pers/AlphaBetaandNowGamma.pdf

There are many things to consider as you approach retirement. Your peace of mind is one of them. By choosing to work with a fiduciary, you're choosing to make sure that money worries won't ever be one of the things keeping you up at night.

Investor Checklist:

Do these three things:

- ✓ Understand how your financial professional gets paid.
- ✓ Work with a fiduciary.
- ✓ Give yourself the advantage of a holistic SWAN retirement plan so that you can keep more of your money and sleep well at night.

ABOUT THE AUTHORS

Market Advisory Group was formed in 2014 by founding partners Danny Goolsby, Larry Kloefkorn, and Matt Goolsby, with the addition of Jonathon McCoy in 2015. When you work with any individual professional at Market Advisory Group, you get the full benefits of a team approach. Each client is brought to the attention of the group who together have over 100 years of experience in all areas of financial planning, including investment services, tactical portfolio management, Medicare, Social Security planning, tax planning, and estate planning. As professionals held to the fiduciary standard, they treat their clients like family, put the client's best interests first, and operate with the utmost transparency and honesty. It is their mission to help investors achieve peace of mind in retirement, and they accomplish this under their near-reverent directive of "protect first, grow second."

Danny Goolsby has been serving the financial needs of families from all parts of Kansas and the Central Plains states since 1985. He realized SS plays a major role in retirement planning and the filing strategy for SS plays a major role in retirement, and your investments and savings only provide a portion of your retirement income. Generally speaking, SS is a component of income stream and your investments supplement the income gap. Danny got serious about customized, holistic planning in 2005 when his mother said to him, "Okay, hotshot, tell me—when is the best time to file for Social Security?" She followed the general advice that it was better to wait and file so that her payment would be higher, but at the age of 68 she was diagnosed with terminal cancer and received less than about a year of her benefits. As the group's leading expert on the Social Security system, Danny takes this planning very seriously for every client who works with Market Advisory Group.

Larry Kloefkorn is a lifelong friend and colleague of Danny's who began working in the financial services industry in 2002, after decades of ministry service in Wichita. He considers it his natural calling to work with people and help them to live better lives. His motto is to try to do the usual unusually well so that he can provide people with something they can depend on. When he talks numbers, he tends to under promise and over deliver.

Matt Goolsby literally grew up in the industry as the son of a financial advisor. He officially entered the business in 2004, in order to follow in his father's footsteps, and serves as a licensed life and health agent acting as a fiduciary. He gains the most satisfaction from helping clients who are not getting the kind of service they deserve, and it's their sincere gratitude that he finds most rewarding.

Jonathon McCoy serves as the lead advisor in the Kansas City metro offices. As a licensed securities agent, he didn't enter the industry from the brokerage side or as a life insurance agent, but rather, he was baptized by fire and serves as an independent investment advisor. He witnessed family members experience significant loss due to buy-and-hold investment strategies in the past, and at Market Advisory Group has found a better way to manage his clients' accounts by serving as a fiduciary.

The End. We hope you have enjoyed this financial educational publication brought to you by the Market Advisory Group. For additional information or to reach out to one of our advisors, find us at https://marketadvisorygroup.com/.

Graphics Copyright:

Nagy-Bagoly Arpad
https://www.123rf.com/profile_lightkeeper

lightkeeper / 123RF Stock Photo
 https://www.123rf.com/profile_lightkeeper

Andrei Krauchuk
https://www.123rf.com/profile_rastudio

Padsaworn Wannakarn
https://www.123rf.com/profile_birdigol

Samuraitop
https://www.123rf.com/profile_samuraitop

Jorgen McLeman
https://www.123rf.com/profile_jorgenmac

kittitee pangwang
https://www.123rf.com/profile_bobaa22

Sira Anamwong
https://www.123rf.com/profile_siraanamwong

Wissanu Mushtaprate
https://www.123rf.com/profile_wisaanu99